Germano Vera Cruz

The relationship between skin color and beauty in Mozambique

Germano Vera Cruz

The relationship between skin color and beauty in Mozambique

Book based on scientific research

ScienciaScripts

Imprint
Any brand names and product names mentioned in this book are subject to trademark, brand or patent protection and are trademarks or registered trademarks of their respective holders. The use of brand names, product names, common names, trade names, product descriptions etc. even without a particular marking in this work is in no way to be construed to mean that such names may be regarded as unrestricted in respect of trademark and brand protection legislation and could thus be used by anyone.

Cover image: www.ingimage.com

This book is a translation from the original published under ISBN 978-613-9-62458-4.

Publisher:
Sciencia Scripts
is a trademark of
Dodo Books Indian Ocean Ltd. and OmniScriptum S.R.L publishing group

120 High Road, East Finchley, London, N2 9ED, United Kingdom
Str. Armeneasca 28/1, office 1, Chisinau MD-2012, Republic of Moldova, Europe
Printed at: see last page
ISBN: 978-620-7-72741-4

Index

To my late father, Joaquim, who gave me a passion for knowledge. To my late mother, Luisa, who instilled in me selflessness.

Thanks

My thanks go to Amélie Humeau, Vanessa Emilia Walters, Jena Mussa Sauji and Fénita Manuel Mahendra for their help in carrying out the research on which this book is based.

Preface

The recent publication of the results of scientific research on the "impact of skin color on an individual's appreciation of physical beauty in Mozambique" has aroused great interest in the national press, the public in general and the academic community in particular.

Interest and curiosity were joined by a certain amount of controversy. Meanwhile, many people were looking for the study to read it in full. I replied that the study existed, but in English. So a lot of people asked me to translate it into Portuguese and publish it in the form of a book they could read.

Therefore, it was not my initial intention to publish this research in the form of a book. Written in the form of a scientific article, the study was intended to be published in an international scientific journal.

Given the demand, I decided to translate and publish it. However, in order to make it intellectually accessible to the greatest number of interested parties, I decided, unlike the original article, to simplify the statistical treatment of the data and use more common language.

Furthermore, I think that publishing this research in the form of a book could respond to an academic need. In fact, Mozambican university students complain that the scientific books they have access to in Portuguese are more theoretical than practical and, above all, report on research carried out in Western countries whose reality is different from that to which they are subjected.

Furthermore, this book, written in a didactic way and strictly following the canons recognized by the international scientific community, should also be seen as a model that students can draw on when they want to do and write a scientific research paper.

Controversy

I would like to take this opportunity to respond to the controversy raised when the results of this survey were released.

Two factors, I think, are at the root of the controversy: a *misunderstanding* and *discontent*.

Let's start with the misunderstanding.

The results of this study should be seen as an observation. It is not an affirmation of an absolute and uncontextualized truth. And, obviously, they do not necessarily reflect the opinion of their author.

In fact, in the interviews I gave to various media outlets, I said four things:

The first is that the results of my research indicate that, for the vast majority of the 500 children who took part in the study, light skin color is a determining beauty criterion, and that consequently they tend to consider light-skinned women to be generally more beautiful than dark-skinned women, when comparing women of more or less equivalent physical appearance. This is a fact.

The second is that from the results of this survey, we can generalize and say that most Mozambican children tend to consider light-skinned women to be more beautiful than dark-skinned women, when other physical aspects are more or less equivalent. This is an extrapolation.

The third is that this was not only the assessment of children, but also that of adults, taking into account the fact that children's preferences are generally the result of adult influence. This is a logical and psychosocial deduction.

The fourth is that overall, in Mozambican society, there is a tendency to positively appreciate light-skinned people and to negatively appreciate dark-skinned people, when compared to each other. He also said that this was not just a clear trend in our society today. It is also an apparently pan-cultural trend.

I hope that what I have just said will clarify the understanding of the results of my research, eliminating misunderstandings.

As far as dissatisfaction is concerned, I would say the following.

First, it's that thing: This doesn't suit me, so it doesn't exist. This shouldn't be, then it isn't.

But things are what they are, regardless of our will or our discontent. And we mustn't confuse "what is" with "what should be" or "what we would like it to be".

As far as I'm concerned, I prefer to be realistic.

Secondly, there are the "unconscious" or pseudo-unconscious. They have an intimate intuition of the truth. However, they don't like it to be spoken openly. And on they go, exchanging cat for hare. They say that this is racism, or that it will create racism.

I reply that if it is racism, it was racism before and it will be racism afterwards. Hiding (repressing) or revealing (raising awareness) doesn't change the essence.

As far as I'm concerned, I prefer to exorcise my "demons" rather than pretend I don't have any.

Finally. In this category of the disgruntled, there are also the complexed and some overweight people.

The results of this study are irritating for the complexed people, those who would like to be "white" and not "black", because they see themselves in the *mirror,* just like them.

However, I want to console them. By assuring them that they are many and not alone. Indeed, many black people would like to be white; among white people, many brunettes would like to be blond; many women would like to be men[1] ; many poor people would like to be rich; many ugly people would like to be beautiful. Because, in general, we prefer what is advantageous to what is disadvantageous!

Many of us who have curly hair would like to have it straight (the fashion for straight artificial hair practiced by our black women is proof of this!); and among whites, many of us who have black hair would like to have it blonde (the fashion for dyeing our hair blonde practiced by men and especially brunette women is also proof of this).

Nobody wants to be socially disadvantaged. And, in a way, it's normal to want to have the characteristics that confer (real or supposed) psychological, social and, above all, economic advantages.

This also explains why some overweight people are irritated by the results of the study. They fear unreasonable jealousy, or social awareness where they might lose out. Not to mention an uncomfortable self-blame, which is common in such cases and difficult to accept.

I'd like to console them, and so would they. They're not guilty of being preferred. Of course, as long as they don't abuse their perks!

Perhaps I should end by summarizing my ideas in a phrase from the famous French sociologist, Pierre Bourdieu: One of the things that makes domination tragic is that it is often exercised with the complicity of the dominated.

Cruel truth!

And here's a question for your homework: In your experience, dear reader, have you

---

1 In societies where men are socially advantaged and women socially disadvantaged.

never seen a situation where some blacks discriminate against other blacks in favor of whites? Have you never seen some poor people disregarding other poor people in favor of the rich?

Answer honestly and to yourself.

GERMANO VERA CRUZ, Maputo, October 2008

Introduction

This study aims to verify the existence or not, in our society, of the consistent tendency (attitude) to prefer light skin color (pro-light skin tendency) over dark skin color (anti-dark skin tendency). Is it true that, in Mozambique, light-skinned people are generally considered more beautiful or physically attractive than dark-skinned people, when other aspects of physical appearance are controlled?

This is the question that motivated this research.

We also want to know what correlation there is between certain variables such as gender, age, socio-cultural level and the pro-skinny trend, in terms of appreciation of physical beauty.

This study seems necessary for the following reasons:

1. In several African and Western countries, following a practice that began in the United States in the first half of the 20th century, an increasing number of black women and men are taking health risks by lightening their skin with the help of chemical products in the form of ointments (M'bemba-Ndoumba, 2004)[2] . Those who do so think that with light skin they will be more attractive or more desirable.

Naturally, this phenomenon affects women more than men.

"In the same way that most Western men prefer blonde women, most African men prefer light women, because they find them more attractive than dark women," a young Mozambican university student told us, after admitting that she had been applying a certain cream for two years in order to have lighter skin.

Some women cite social pressure as the decisive factor that led them to depigment their skin: "As you can see, I have very dark skin. Well, ever since I was a child,

---

2 In recent years, these facts have also been reported in the Western press.

some members of my family have made unpleasant comments about it. As for my curly hair, the managers of my company expressly asked me to wear it down in order to better represent the good reputation of the institution. So I decided to do both, lighten my skin and straighten my hair," explained another young Mozambican woman.

2. In Mozambique, we can see that, for example, most of the women who appear on the advertising posters of large companies or large commercial establishments have light skin color[3] . Naturally, this contrasts with the physical and demographic reality of the country. In fact, most Mozambican women (certainly more than 90%) have dark skin.

3. In everyday conversation, in music or in popular music videos, Mozambicans show a preference for light skin color over dark skin color. In fact, light skin color seems to be the main criterion for female beauty[4] .

We could multiply examples that indicate the existence, in Mozambican society, of a more favorable attitude towards light-skinned people compared to dark-skinned people. But as many and as obvious as these examples are, perhaps they are no more than impressions. Hence the need for scientific (methodological and objective) research to ascertain the impact of light skin color on a person's appreciation of physical beauty in Mozambique.

Let's clear up any misunderstandings immediately. Our purpose here is not to criticize. We don't intend to criticize anyone, let alone make a social demand.

---

3 See attachment.

4 In this regard, we can quote a song by Joaquim Macuacua which goes something like this: "You're swinging because you're beautiful and clear". In the rural areas of the province of Inhambane, where I was born, when a woman gives birth to a very pale child, it is common to hear comments like: "Oh, with that pale little daughter of yours, you could make a good profit by marrying her off to a *majonejone* (Mozambicans who go to work in the mines of neighboring South Africa and therefore have a relatively better material condition)". Another example: you often hear people being congratulated on having returned to their country with relatively clear skin after a long stay in a foreign country where it is very cold in reverse.

We are fully aware, then, that preferences are what they are, often independently of our conscious will. What's more, it seems to us that this tendency has become socio-cultural, no longer just individual. In other words, it has been *socially constructed*. So who would we blame? Society?[5]

What matters to us is whether light-skinned people are in fact generally considered more beautiful or physically attractive than dark-skinned people. As for the causes, we'll discuss them later, if the results of our research warrant it.

It should be noted that the study reported in this book was carried out in 2008. Since then, I have conducted several other studies (e.g., Vera Cruz, 2012; Vera Cruz, 2013; Vera Cruz & Mullet, 2014; Vera Cruz, 2015; Vera Cruz, 2016; Vera Cruz, 2017; Vera Cruz, 2018) on the impact of skin color on an individual's appreciation of beauty. These studies have been published in international scientific journals. We advise the reader to read them. You can search for some of these articles by typing *Germano Vera Cruz Researchgate* into the Google search engine.

---

5 It should also be said that preferring light-skinned people does not necessarily mean discriminating against (in the sense of harming for the sake of) dark-skinned people. Although this sometimes happens consciously or unconsciously. Therefore, one of the merits of this type of study is to make people aware so that their private "racial preferences" don't turn into racial discrimination.

Chapter I

Previous studies

Previous studies of adults and children in the United States, Western Europe and Asia have shown that there is a greater tendency to be white than black, and a greater tendency to be light-skinned than dark-skinned.

In general, the results of these studies do not vary with gender, but they do vary significantly with the age and ethnic origin of the participants.

Furthermore, the fact that almost all of the above-mentioned surveys, carried out on different continents, came to the same conclusions, gave rise to the idea that the pro-white and pro-light-skin trends are pan-cultural trends.

B+/P-

Thus, the pan-cultural tendency to appreciate the color white positively (B+) and to attribute a negative connotation to the color black (P-) has been tested in adults in several countries (Best, Naylor & Williams, 1978; Best, Field & Williams, 1979; Dent, 1976; Iwawaki, Sonoo, Williams & Best, 1978; Neto & Williams, 1997; Campos & Neto, 2001).

In addition, Adams and Osgood (1973) observed that young adults from all 23 linguistic-cultural groups they studied in America, Europe and Asia used the word "white" more positively than the word "black".

Williams and Morland (1976) obtained the same results after studying seven American and Oriental groups. However, this trend proved to be relatively weak in the groups made up of black individuals.

As for children's attitudes towards white and black, this has been studied in the

United States, several European countries and Japan, using a research instrument known as the *Color Meaning Test II* (CMT II; Williams, Boswell & Best, 1975)[6] .

Other studies carried out in the United States by Williams and Morland (1976) showed the existence of a pro-white/anti-black tendency (B+/P-) in pre-school Euro-American and African-American children, with the same tendency decreasing in groups made up of black individuals.

The B+/P- propensity has also been found in children aged 5 and 6 in England and Scotland (Dent, 1976), France and Italy (Best, Naylor & Williams, 1975), Germany (Best, Field & Williams, 1976), Japan (Iwawaki, Sonoo, Williams & Best, 1978) and Portugal (Neto & Williams, 1997; Neto & Paiva, 1998; Campos & Neto, 2001).

PC+/PE-

Parallel to the study of the B+/P- trend, using a research instrument called *Preschool Racial Attitude Measure II* (PRAM II;

Williams, Best, Boswell, Mattson & Graves, 1975)[7] , several researchers have carried out studies with the aim of verifying the possibility of the existence, in children, of a propensity to appreciate light-skinned people more positively than dark-skinned people.

Thus, the pro-light skin/anti-dark skin trend (PC+/PE-) has been detected several times in Euro-American and African-American children of pre-school age (Williams

---

6 CMT II takes the form of an interview based on stories and pictures. The child is told a story and given 24 opportunities to choose between the figure of a white animal and the figure of a black animal which, for example, would best embody the *bad* animal or the *kind animal* (there are 12 positive and 21 negative adjectives) evoked in the story.

7 The PRAM II is an instrument that proposes a dichotomous choice to measure the racial attitudes of children aged 3 to 9. In its original form, it consists of 36 items: 24 items on racial attitudes and 12 items on gender roles. For each racial attitude item, the child is told a story that contains a qualifying adjective and is then asked to choose between a light-skinned human figure and a dark-skinned human figure that would best correspond to the person described in the story (e.g. Which is the *bad* man? Which is the *wonderful* woman?).

& Morland, 1976).

This trend has also been observed in pre-school children in France and Italy (Best, Naylor & Williams, 1975), Germany (Best, Field & Williams, 1976), Japan (Iwawaki, Sonoo, Williams & Best, 1978) and Portugal (Neto & Williams, 1997).

Chapter II

This study

While there are several studies on the appreciation of white and black colors, on the appreciation of light skin in relation to dark skin, carried out in America, Europe and Asia, as far as we know, few studies have been carried out on the same subject in Africa.

For this reason, we believe that this study, carried out in Mozambique, is of particular interest.

However, it is important to point out that even though our study is inspired by the previous studies described above, and can even be considered a continuation of them, it differs from the previous ones in terms of its precise objectives (to verify the relationship between skin color and the evaluation of beauty) and the scientific method used (as we will see below).

1. Hypothesis

After the observations we made in the introduction above, we will formulate our hypotheses in a clear way:

a) We hope that the results of this study confirm the observations that, in Mozambique, light skin color is a beauty criterion that determines physical attractiveness and, consequently, the existence of the pro-light-skin trend.

b) Furthermore, we do not think that there will be a significant difference between the response of male and female subjects, nor will there be a significant difference in this type of attitude depending on the socio-cultural level of the participants.

c) On the other hand, we predicted a significant impact of the variables Age and

Educational level: The higher the subject's age and educational level, the lower the preference for light skin color (even if in this case of the figure, the choice of light color remains the majority).

In our opinion, the factor that explains this last prediction is the following: With advancing age and educational level, individuals acquire critical thinking skills and judgment (the tendency to self-censorship and convenience speech also increases), which is likely to temper the spontaneous and "unconscious" tendencies that are generally involved in all preferential choices.

2. Method

a) Research tool

How can we verify objectively, that is, clearly, whether or not there is a pro-light-skin and anti-dark-skin tendency in the appreciation of beauty in Mozambique?

This question troubled us for months.

Well. I went through several possibilities.

To build a hybrid instrument, capable of verifying both female and male appreciation of beauty?

Practical difficulties led us to decide to focus our research only on female beauty.

Indeed, as we saw above, the problem of lightening the skin through the use of cosmetics affects women more than men (M'Bemba-Ndoumba, 2004). On the other hand, light skin color seems to be the main criterion of beauty for women. Perhaps this is because, traditionally, the issue of physical beauty affects women first and foremost, whatever the country or culture[8] .

Once this point has been resolved, what next?

We thought we'd take a photo of a beautiful black girl, a photo of a beautiful mixed race girl and a photo of a beautiful white girl. We would present these photos to the research subjects, one by one, asking them to choose the most beautiful of the three.

But how can we choose the three beautiful girls in such a way that they are all indisputably beautiful? "Nothing is more debatable than beauty!" we would object.

"Then let's take pictures of three famous models from around the world and the problem will be solved," we thought.

But how do you make the beauty of the three models (black, mixed and white) exactly equivalent? How can this be achieved with three different people, from different "races", so famous are they?

These considerations led us to a single solution. A solution that was both practical, fair and objective. We had to take a photo of a single girl. And from it, make two more versions. If the original photo was of a black girl, we should make a "mixed version" and a "white version" from it. And so on.

Let's get to work. For pragmatic reasons, we decided to take a photo of a mixed race girl and use an information program to create a black version and a white version.

So we chose some candidates, students of mine at Eduardo Mondlane University, who agreed to pose for a photo shoot. The digital photos were taken by a professional photographer.

---

8 "While a man must be rich and powerful to be attractive, a woman must be beautiful to be attractive." This is how we can summarize the results of the studies carried out in this regard by the famous American anthropologist Helen Fischer (2008).

We then chose the photo of one of the seven candidates. This choice was made according to criteria of technical practicality. By this we mean that we chose the photo of the girl whose skin color was closest to the average between "dark" and "white". Indeed, it would be difficult to darken a very light skin color and equally difficult to lighten a very dark skin color.

Once the choice had been made, we sent the photo to a computer technician in France, who *darkened* the skin color of the girl in the original photo (mixed) to obtain the "photo-girl-black" version and *lightened* the skin color of the girl in the original photo to obtain the "photo-girl-white" version. These two versions were thus added to the original photo baptized "photo-girl-mixed".

Thus, our instrument for verifying the pro-light skin tendency, our research instrument, that is to say, our data collection instrument, was already in place: Three versions of the same photograph. These three versions are exclusively identical. The only difference between them is the lighter and lighter skin color of the girl in them.

b)   **Test**

To whom should we apply our instrument to verify the existence or not of a tendency (attitude) more favorable to light skin, compared to dark skin, in the appreciation of female beauty in Mozambique?

In other words: Which group of people should be asked to take part in our study?

Right from the start, we realized that teenagers and adults would see that they were photos of the same girl. And naturally, they would ask: "Why?". This would make it more likely that they would anticipate the researcher's presumed intentions by answering out *of convenience.*

It was this reflection that led us to decide to apply this data collection instrument only to children aged 4 (already of school age) to 11.

In fact, at the beginning, this decision was a kind of postulate to be tested, before the final decision was made. In fact, we postulated the ideal age on the basis of the theories of the development of human capacities, cognitive and social skills conceived by Piaget and Inhelder (1966), as well as their followers.

According to these theories, the abilities mentioned above develop progressively from birth to adulthood. In this way, it seemed to us that children under the age of 12, at least the vast majority of them, would not realize that they were photos of the same girl.

We're also thinking about another aspect. Children under the age of 12 (we set 12 as the probable age of transition between childhood and adolescence), in general, have not yet developed the tendency to make value judgments and criticize their own preferences or spontaneous choices, which could lead them to try to anticipate the researcher's objectives or expectations in order to go *for* or *against* them.

In fact, the different tests we carried out confirmed our initial postulate. No child under the age of 12 made a reflection that indicated that they had noticed that they were photographs of the same person. The 12-year-olds sometimes figured it out, although not always. But teenagers aged 13 and over almost automatically unraveled the "mystery" of the photos. Some of them even exclaimed: "It's the same person, with a different skin color! How and why did you do this?".

The most compromising thing is that some of these teenagers aged 13 and over (at least three of them) made critical remarks against the children who chose the "white girl" as the prettiest of them all: "What! Is this the prettiest one for you? Can't you see that it's the same person in these photos? Of course, you chose this one because she's the lightest, didn't you? You're black, so you should choose this black one too...", raged a 14-year-old teenager.

Finally. The different tests carried out on 37 subjects (we went to meet the children in the street and sometimes at their homes) should also serve as a basis for checking the consistency of the answers given by the participants in the research.

To do this, we gave the same subject the same verification instrument twice at varying time intervals (a few minutes, a day, or two days apart). We also changed the size of the photos presented to the participants (10x15 or 20x25).

This is how we were able to see that, overall, the children's response was consistent at 93%.

And so we validated our research instrument which, let's remember, was completely invented by us.

c) **Sample and procedure**

The research was carried out in May and June 2008 in three primary schools in the city and province of Maputo. Two schools in the city of Maputo (Escola Primària 7 de Setembro and Escola Primària Felipe Samuel Magaia) and one in the district of Boane (Escola Primària de Campoane), the latter attended mostly by children from low socio-cultural backgrounds.

A total of 500 children took part in the study: 258 (52%) males and 242 (48%) females; 259 (52%) from low socio-cultural backgrounds and 241 (48%) from medium and high socio-cultural backgrounds (the socio-cultural backgrounds of the subjects were determined solely on the basis of the children's place of origin - semi-rural areas for the low socio-cultural backgrounds, for example).

The age of the participants ranges from 4 to 11 years. Based on theories of child development, we subdivided the subjects into three age groups: 4 to 6 years = 198 subjects, 7 to 8 years = 171 subjects and 9 to 11 years = 131 subjects.

The participants' schooling ranged from *first* to *seventh* grade. Because of the inherent need to analyze the data collected, we regrouped the subjects according to their belonging to the following school levels: 1-2 (first - second class) = 281 subjects, 3-4 (third - fourth class) = 199 subjects and 5-7 (fifth - seventh class) = 20 subjects.

As far as the procedure is concerned, we first sent a letter to the heads of the selected schools, asking for permission to carry out a survey on "children's cognitive development". In fact, we felt it was important to keep the actual purpose of the research a secret, so that it wouldn't influence the results in any way.

On the agreed day, we went to the previously identified educational establishments. My assistant and I entered the classroom. We sat next to a desk that had been prepared and placed at the back of the room.

We invited the children one by one. The main question we asked was: "You see these three pictures here. Look at them. There are three girls. So tell us, in your opinion, which of these three girls is the most beautiful?".

In general, the child would point with their finger to the girl they thought was the prettiest, saying: "This is the one".

In order to prevent the children from influencing each other, we systematically separated the children who had already answered from the children who were waiting for their turn. What's more, we constantly changed the order in which the photos were placed on the card.

Chapter III

Results

1. General results

Table 1.

Skin color	Number of participants
White	314
Mixed	126
Black	60
Total	500

The table above shows the quantitative distribution of the participants' choice (preference in terms of beauty) among the three possible choices.

Reading it from right to left and from top to bottom, we see that out of a total of 500 participants, 314 chose the *white girl*[9] as the most beautiful; 126 participants chose the *mixed girl,* and only 60 individuals considered the *black girl to* be the most beautiful of all.

At the same time, as the circle-shaped graph below shows, the percentage distribution of the subjects' choices was as follows: 63% of the subjects chose the white girl, 25% chose the mixed race girl, and only 12% chose the black girl as the most beautiful.

---

9 From now on, for ease of use, we will use the terms *white girl, mixed girl* and *black girl* respectively instead of "white photo-girl", "mixed photo-girl" and "black photo-girl".

Graph 1.

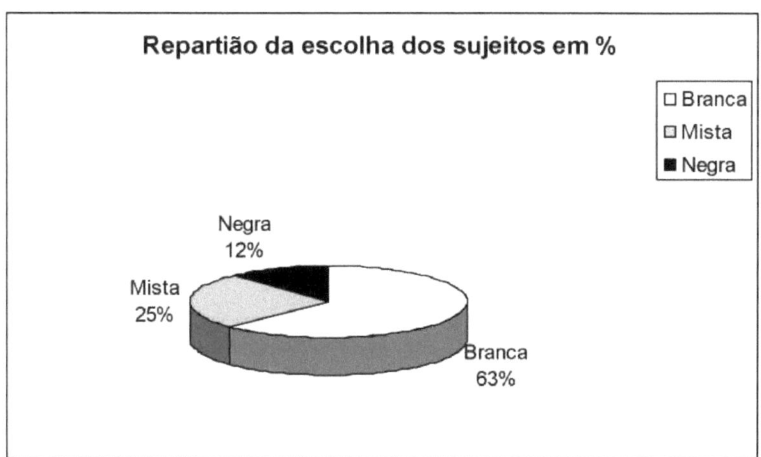

2. Variation in results according to gender

Graph 2.

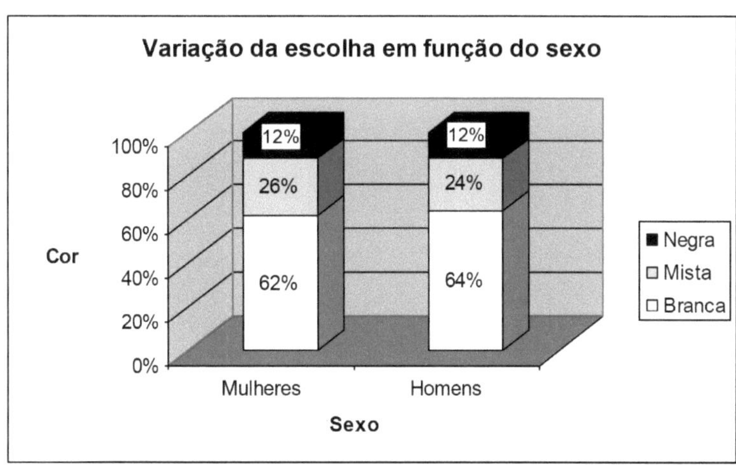

The graph above compares the choice made by the female subjects with the choice made by the male subjects.

It shows that 62% of the women chose the white girl, 26% chose the mixed race girl and 12% chose the black girl. With regard to the male subjects, 64% of them chose the white girl, 24% chose the mixed girl and 12% chose the black girl.

In light of these results, we can say that there is no significant difference between the choice made by female children and the choice made by male children[10]. In fact, the difference is only 2% when it comes to the choice of the white girl and the mixed girl. The percentage of preference for the black girl (12%) is identical for both genders.

3.   Variation in results according to socio-cultural level

---

10 This inference is the result of our X2 tests. Furthermore, as this is a popular book, we have decided not to include complex statistics in it. Readers wishing to find out more about the statistical results should read the scientific article (Vera Cruz, 2013) published on this research in the *Journal of Psychology in Africa.*

Graph 3.

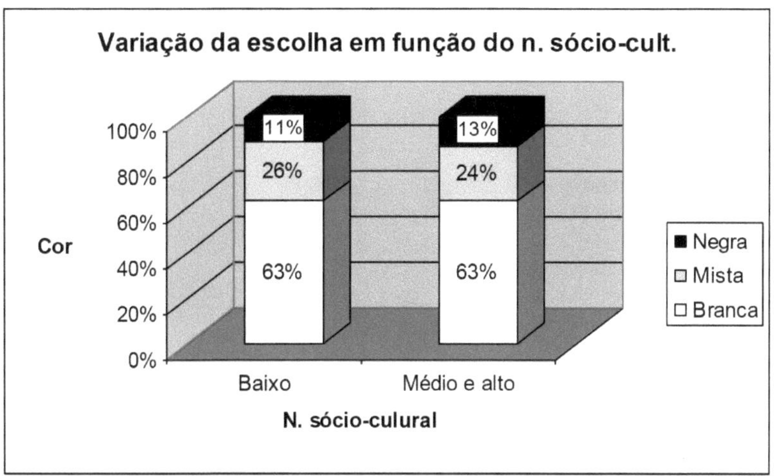

As you can see in the graph above, we have calculated the differential choice made by the two socio-cultural groups discriminated against.

Thus, 63% of the *low socio-cultural level* subjects chose the white girl, 26% chose the mixed race girl and 11% chose the black girl.

At the same time, we see that 63% of the participants from the *medium and high socio-cultural levels* chose the white girl, 24% chose the mixed girl and 13% chose the black girl.

We can therefore see that in this case the difference between the choice made by the subjects in the two groups is not significant either. In fact, there is equality when it comes to the choice of the white girl (63% in both socio-cultural groups). The difference in the other two choices between the two groups is only 2%.

4. Variation in results according to age group

Graph 4.

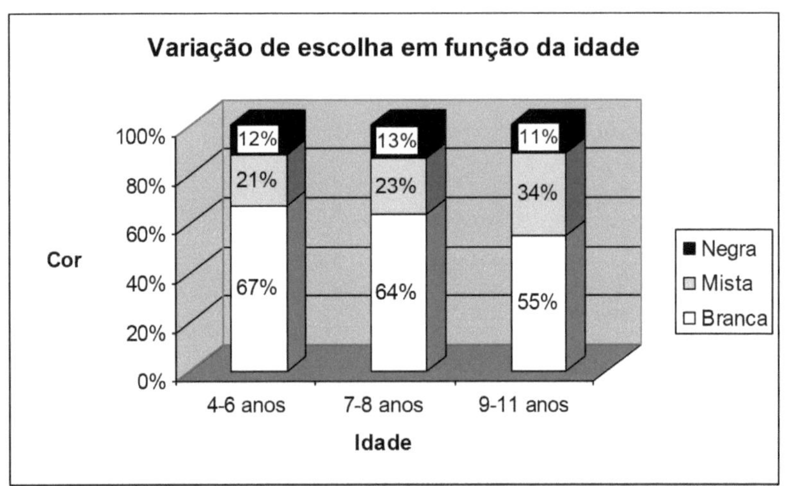

The graph above shows, as a percentage, the choice made by the three age groups we've broken down (4-6 years, 7-8 years and 9-11 years).

Looking at the graph, we can see that the percentage of subjects who chose the white girl decreases as age increases. This decrease is significant from the second age group onwards: from 64% to 55% (9% difference).

At the same time, the choice of the mixed girl increases with age. This increase is significant from the second group: from 23% to 34% (11% difference).

The choice of the black girl, when we move from one group to another, is stable. In fact, with a variation of 12%, 13% and 11%, we don't see a significant change in attitude when we move from one group to another.

5. Variation in results according to school level

Graph 5.

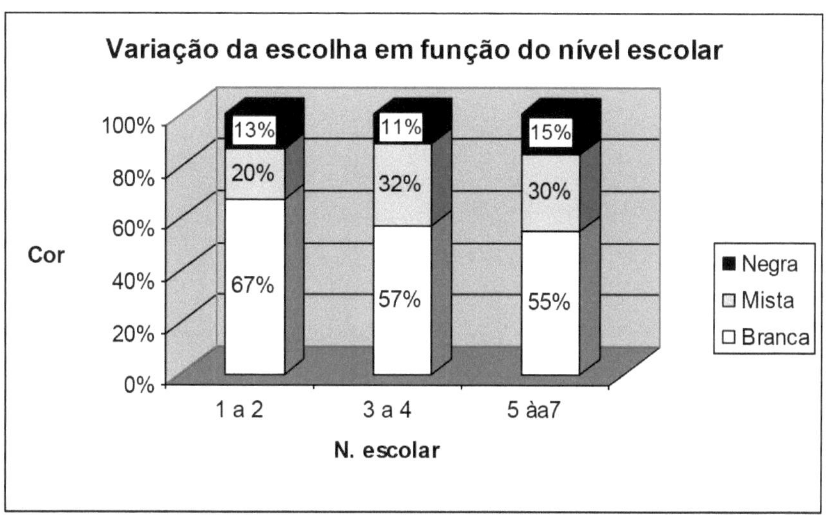

The graph above shows, as a percentage, the choice made by the subjects of the three school levels we have broken down (1-2, 3-4, 5-7 years of study).

We can then see that the percentage of subjects who chose the white girl drops as the participants' level of education increases. This drop is significant from the first to the second group: from 67% to 57% respectively (10% difference).

At the same time, we see that the choice of the mixed girl increases significantly when we move from the first to the second school group.

The percentage of black girls chosen does not change significantly when we move from one school level to the next. In fact, with a successive variation of 13%, 11% and 15%, we don't see a significant change in attitude.

Chapter IV

Discussion

In this chapter, we will first examine the results set out above, relating them to the starting hypotheses of this study and to the results of previous studies. Secondly, we will try to interpret the results of our study and indicate prospects for future studies.

1. Confirmation of hypotheses

-       The first hypothesis we put forward is that, in Mozambique, there is a tendency to favor light skin color over dark skin color when it comes to appreciating female physical beauty.

The results of our study confirm this hypothesis. Indeed, of the 500 subjects who took part in the study, 314 (63%) indicated the photo of the girl with the lightest skin (white girl) as being the most beautiful of all[11] .

The second highest vote-getter, so to speak, was the relatively light-haired girl (Miss Mixed), who received 126 votes (i.e. 25%).

The dark-skinned girl (black girl) was chosen as the most beautiful of all by only 60 participants (12%), out of a total of 500 individuals questioned.

Thus, these results agree with the pro-light skin/anti-dark skin trend (PC+/PE+) found in several studies carried out on European, Euro-American and African-American children, as well as Asian children (Best, Naylor & Williams, 1975; Best, Field & Williams, 1979; Dent, 1976; Iwawaki, Sonoo, Williams & Best, 1978; Neto & Williams, 1997; Campos & Neto, 2001).

---

11 Let's remember that the research was carried out using photos of the same girl and that we lightened and darkened the skin color to obtain three different versions: "photo-girl-white", "photo-girl-mixed", "photo-girl-black".

- The second hypothesis we put forward is that there would be no significant difference between the choice of female subjects and the choice of male subjects, on the one hand; nor would there be a significant difference between the choice of subjects from different socio-cultural backgrounds.

The results of this study also confirm this hypothesis. In fact, the statistical treatment of the data shows that the quantitative difference between the choice made by women and the choice made by men does not exceed 2%. The quantitative difference between the choice made by participants of low social level and that made by participants of medium and high socio-cultural level also does not exceed 2%.

These results are in line with those observed in previous studies carried out in the United States, Europe and Asia (Best, Naylor & Williams, 1975; Best, Field & Williams, 1979; Dent, 1976; Iwawaki, Sonoo, Williams & Best, 1978; Neto & Williams, 1997; Campos & Neto, 2001).

- The third and final hypothesis we put forward is that the choice of light skin color would decrease as the age and educational level of the subjects increased; and the choice of dark skin color would increase in the same proportion.

This hypothesis came true. But it was only partially true. In fact, the data from our study shows that the choice of the white girl, even though it continues to be higher in all cases, decreases significantly as the age and educational level of the participants increases. However, contrary to our predictions, the choice of the black girl did not change in the opposite direction.

This means that the quantitative drop in the choice of the white girl as the age and educational level of the subjects increases, only favored the mixed girl and not the black girl. Which perhaps goes to show how inexorably the participants tend to prefer light skin colors!

This aspect of our study is both in line with the results of some previous studies and at odds with others. Indeed, some previous studies show that the PC+/PE- trend increases with age (Doyle, Aboud & Sufrategui, 1992), and other studies show the opposite (Campos & Neto, 2001).

2.   Interpretation

-     The overall agreement between the results of our study, carried out in Mozambique (Africa), and previous studies carried out on other continents confirms the pan-cultural nature of the PC+/PE- trend.

The pan-culturalism of this trend divides scientists as to its interpretation.

Some see this as a pretext for positioning themselves in favor of an *evolutionist* (*biologist*) interpretation linked to the diurnal nature of *Homo sapiens* (Williams & Morland, 1976). Indeed, proponents of this thesis note that the human retina has poor night vision, which leads it to naturally prefer "light" to "shadow", and consequently to prefer light colors to dark colors (Williams & Morland, 1976).

This theory is reinforced by the fact that some researchers have found, in the majority of children studied in various Western and Asian countries, a positive correlation between the pro-light skin/anti-dark skin tendency score

(PC+/PE-) and the pro-white/anti-black color trend score (B+/P-) (Williams & Morland, 1976).

Other scientists, on the other hand, believe that the apparent Universality of the PC+/PE- and B+/P- tendencies is the result of *social learning (social constructivism) of the* cultural model and point of view of the dominant peoples (Whites) since the European Colonial expansions (campos & Neto, 2001).

In most parts of the world, we can summarize this interpretation as the result of the colonial heritage and its ideology of systematic contempt for the black "race": the lighter the skin color of an individual, the more likely they are to occupy privileged positions in the social hierarchy (Sméralda, 2005).

This is how the inherent (intrinsic?) value of light skin color is constructed (social constructivism), a color that is thus generally more advantageous than dark skin color.

Unfortunately, it is not possible for us to resurrect our African ancestors, the Aborigines of Australia and other black peoples who existed in the world without contact with "white domination" and its ideology of the superiority of their race, to ask them if they generally had this tendency to appreciate their lighter-skinned counterparts more. Indeed, if this were possible, then we would have to give the evolutionist interpretation unreserved credit.

(Incidentally, it seems that when the blond type appeared in Europe between 11,000 and 20,000 years ago, due to a genetic modification caused by dietary deficiencies, contemporaries immediately preferred it to the then more common brunette type [Pitman, 2003]).

In any case, it seems to us that the biologist interpretation and the social interpretation should not be considered exclusive of each other, as most of the scientists we have highlighted above tend to do. In our opinion, the two interpretations can coexist and even complement each other.

That said, we lean more in favor of the theory of social learning or so-called social constructivism. Indeed, we are of the opinion that the pro-skinny trend has emerged prominently in individuals in almost all societies as a result of the assimilation, conscious or unconscious, of the point of view conveyed by the culture and civilization that has dominated the world for more than five centuries.

It's enough to note two facts that, in our opinion, are culturally decisive:

The first is that Western languages are used as the main languages[12] in the official teaching and learning system (as well as official languages) in most countries around the world. However, these languages contain elements (e.g. expressions such as *black humor, a dark day,* etc.) that value light colors and depreciate dark colors [13] . The second is that the majority of television and film programs broadcast in most countries, which are likely to have a strong identifying impact, are made and embodied by people of the white "race".

Thus, it seems more than obvious to us that these two factors, not to mention many others, cannot not have an impact on the system of representations of the societies under their yoke.

- Some researchers, whose studies show that the PC+/PE- tendency increases with age, consider that this same factor goes in favor of the social learning theory (Campos & Neto, 2001), when it comes to explaining the panculturalism of this propensity: As they grow up, children assimilate the dominant models.

Other researchers, whose studies show that the PC+/PE- tendency decreases with age, also estimate that this fact is in favor of the social learning theory interpretation (Doyle, Aboud & Sufrategui, 1992): Prejudices decrease with increasing age.

We think that in this case too, these two positions should not be seen as contradictory and exclusive of each other. In fact, the way we see it, prejudices can either decrease or increase with age, depending on the individual, the situation and, above all, the type of prejudice.

---

12 Language is of great cultural importance in that it is the main vehicle for communication (socialization), for identifying a people, and it is ultimately what structures thought.

13 Each cultural creation contains, in addition to its physical form, the code of conduct and interaction that made it possible, and which also conditions the actions of the new generations that use it. In the same way, language contains representations and clippings of "worlds" bequeathed by culture, and this is how representations and visions of the world are transmitted from one generation to the next.

What seems to invariably increase with age is the tendency to self-censor. Younger children are, so to speak, more "authentic". They tend to be more sincere than their elders in publicly expressing their preferences. This is because they have not yet fully integrated a whole social mechanism that will later lead them to self-evaluate their assessments in the light of what is socially convenient to express in certain circumstances, or according to their immediate interest.

The more we advance in age and educational level (in this case, we postulate the acquisition of an ever greater capacity for reflection), the more we tend to give importance, in our statements and in our choices made publicly, to the *imperative of convenience and* the *principle of reality*. This tendency often leads to self-censorship and even bad faith.

It is precisely for this reason that, from the outset, we hypothesized that the choice of the lighter-skinned girl would decrease with increasing age and educational level; and the choice of the darker-skinned girl would increase with increasing age and educational level. As we have seen, this hypothesis was partially verified.

3. Future studies

However, in order to better verify this last hypothesis, it seems necessary to adopt a different research methodology (a different data collection instrument) which would allow the same type of study to be carried out on adolescents and adults. This would allow us to compare the results of such a study with this one carried out on 4-11 year olds.

Furthermore, it would be interesting to carry out this type of study in other regions of Mozambique and in other countries with the same characteristics as ours, with the aim of verifying, for example, whether light-skinned people are more likely to get certain types of jobs.

Or to carry out methodical studies to find out whether light-skinned people are considered more competent or intelligent than dark-skinned people, etc. globally.

34

References

Introduction

M'bemba-Ndoumba, G. (2004). *Ces Noirs qui se blanchissent la peau. La pratique du " maquillage " chez les Congolais*. Paris, France: L'Harmattan.

Vera Cruz, G. (2012). Age, gender and social class influences on skin color preferences among Mozambican children. *Journal of Psychology in Africa, 22*(1), 139-142. doi: 10.1080/14330237.2012.10874532

Vera Cruz, G. (2013). Cross-cultural study of facial beauty. *Journal of Psychology in Africa, 23*(1), 87-90. doi: 10.1080/14330237.2013.10820597

Vera Cruz, G., & Mullet, E. (2014). The impact of skin tone on perceived facial beauty: A two-culture study. *Psychological: International Journal of Methodology and Experimental Psychology, 35(3)*, 729-743.

Vera Cruz, G. (2016). *Sexualité, amour, beauté : Perspectives occidentales vs. Perspectives africaines*. Berlin, Allemagne : Editions Universitaires Européennes.

Vera Cruz, G. (2015). *Sexuality, love and physical attractiveness: Euro-Western vs. Southern Africa perspectives*. Berlin, Germany: LAP Lambert Academic Publishing.

Vera Cruz, G. (2018). The impact of face skin tone vs. face symmetry on perceived facial attractiveness. *The Journal of General Psychology*. doi: 10.1080/00221309.2018.1459452

Vera Cruz, G. (2017). The impact of face skin tone on perceived facial attractiveness: A study realized with an innovative methodology. *The Journal of Social Psychology*. doi: 10.1080/00224545.2017.1419161

Chapter I

Adams, F. M., & Osgood, C. (1973). A cross-cultural study of the affective meanings of color. *Journal of Cross-Cultural Psychology*, 4, 135-156.

Best, D. L., Field, J. T., & Williams, J. E. (1976). Color bias in a sample of young German children. *Journal of Cross-Cultural Psychology*, 6, 390405.

Best, D.L., Naylor, C. E, & Williams, J. E. (1975). Extension of color bias research to young French and Italian children. *Journal of Cross-Cultural Psychology*, 6, 390-405.

Campos, G., & Neto, F. (2001). Children's attitudes towards color and ethnicity Pitman, J. (2003). *Psychology, Education and Culture*, vol. V, 2, 271-287.

Dent, E. (1976). *Evaluative responses of preschool children to the colors black and white*. Unpublished master thesis. Univ. of Strathclyde.

Fischer, H. (2008). *Histoire naturelle de l'amour*. Paris : Hachette.

Iwawaki, S., Sonoo, K., Williams, J. E., & Best, D. L. (1978). Color bias among young Japanese children. Journal of Cross-cultural Psychology, 9, 61-73.

Morland, K. (1958). Racial recognition of nursery school children in Lynchburg, Virginia. *Social Forces*, 37, 132-137.

Neto, F., & Williams, J. E. (1997). Color bias in children revisited : findings from Portugal. *Social Behavior and Personality*, 25(2), 115-122.

Neto, F., & Paiva, L. (1998). Color and racial attitudes in white, black and biracial children. *Social Behavior and Personality*, 6(3), 233-244.

Pereira, M. E., & Lima, M. E. O. (2003). Skin color and cultural change in Portugal and Brazil: a comparative study. *Psicologia, Educaçao e Cultura,* vol. VII, 2, 261-283.

Piaget, J. & Inhelder, B. (1966). *The psychology of children*. Paris, France: PUF.

Pitman, J. (2003). *On Blondes*. New York, NY : Blomsbury.

Sméralda, J. (2005). *Peau noire, cheveux crépus, histoire d'une aliénation*.

Guadeloupe : Jasor.

Williams, J. E., Best, D. L., & Boswell, D. A. (1975). The Measurement of children's racial attitudes in the early school years. *Child Development*, 46, 494-500.

Williams, J. E., Boswell, D. A., & Best, D. L. (1975). Evaluative responses of preschool children to the colors white and black. *Child Development*, 46, 501-508.

Williams, J. E., Best, D. L., Boswell, D. A, Mattson, L. A., & Graves, D. J. (1975). Preschool Racial Attitude Measure II. *Educational and Psychological Measurement*, 35, 3-18.

Williams, J. E., & Morland, J. K. (1976). *Race, color, and the young child*. Chapel Hill, NC : University of North Carolina Press.

Chapter II

M'bemba-Ndoumba, G. (2004). *Ces Noirs qui se blanchissent la peau. La pratique du " maquillage " chez les Congolais*. Paris, France: L'Harmattan.

Piaget, J. & Inhelder, B. (1966). *The psychology of children*. Paris, France: PUF.

Chapter IV

Best, D.L., Naylor, C. E, & Williams, J. E. (1975). Extension of color bias research to young French and Italian children. *Journal of Cross-Cultural Psychology*, 6, 390-405.

Best, D. L., Field, J. T., & Williams, J. E. (1976). Color bias in a sample of young German children. *Journal of Cross-Cultural Psychology*, 6, 390405.

Campos, G., & Neto, F. (2001). Children's attitudes towards color and ethnicity Pitman, J. (2003). *Psychology, Education and Culture*, vol. V, 2, 271-287.

Dent, E. (1976). *Evaluative responses of preschool children to the colors black and white*. Unpublished master thesis. Univ. of Strathclyde.

Iwawaki, S., Sonoo, K., Williams, J. E., & Best, D. L. (1978). Color bias among young Japanese children. Journal of Cross-cultural Psychology, 9, 61-73.

Neto, F., & Williams, J. E. (1997). Color bias in children revisited : findings from Portugal. *Social Behavior and Personality*, 25(2), 115-122.

Neto, F., & Paiva, L. (1998). Color and racial attitudes in white, black and biracial children. *Social Behavior and Personality*, 6(3), 233-244.

Pitman, J. (2003). *On Blondes*. New York, NY : Blomsbury.

Sméralda, J. (2005). *Peau noire, cheveux crépus, histoire d'une aliénation.*

Guadeloupe : Jasor.

Williams, J. E., & Morland, J. K. (1976). *Race, color, and the young child.*

Chapel Hill, NC : University of North Carolina Press.

Annex

Experience A.

Here's an experience that everyone can replicate:

On 27/06/08, at around 2pm, I decided to take the Maputo-Matola route, with the aim of observing all the advertising posters with female figures on them.

In fact, I wanted to count, among the women represented in these posters, those who were light-colored, on the one hand, and those who were dark-colored, on the other.

I then left the Vip Hotel. I followed Avenida 25 de Setembro to the end. Then I took the highway towards Matola. At the same time, I was looking carefully on both sides of the road to see the advertising posters hanging on the walls of buildings, in shop windows and on specially made devices.

Having only taken into account the different advertising posters, here is, in order, the note you can make about the skin color of the women I saw:

Clara/Dark/Clara/Clara/Dark/Clara/Clara/Clara/Clara/Clara/Clara/Clara/Clara/Clara/Dark/Clara.

Which means that, during my journey, I saw 17 advertising posters featuring 17 different women. Of the 17 women, only 4 were dark in color!

Everyone can try this out in Maputo city. You can take the same route or a different one (for example, you can follow avenues 24 de Julho and Eduardo Mondlane, from one end to the other).

The result may not be exactly the same. It may vary depending on the route and the moment. Advertising posters change over time. But there is a good chance that the light-skinned women on them are the majority.

So, isn't that amazing in a country where I'm sure more than 90% of women have dark skin? (x)

Experience B.

Here's another experience that everyone can replicate:

In July 2003, I brought "white race" and "black race" dolls from Europe. I had to bring them from Europe because it was difficult to find black dolls in Mozambique at the time! (It's like the mannequins in the stores: they're all white, at least at the time I'm writing this book [2008]!).

I then asked Mozambican children, aged between 3 and 5, living in the city of Matola, to choose between the "white doll" and the "black doll" that they would like to keep as a present.

The result was as follows:

Of the 14 children questioned, 11 chose the white doll and only 3 chose the black doll.

Naturally, this experience is not of decisive value, since the number of children involved is limited.

However, it can be a basis for formulating hypotheses to be verified in a more comprehensive study such as the one we carried out.

(x)

I want morebooks!

Buy your books fast and straightforward online - at one of world's fastest growing online book stores! Environmentally sound due to Print-on-Demand technologies.

Buy your books online at
www.morebooks.shop

Kaufen Sie Ihre Bücher schnell und unkompliziert online – auf einer der am schnellsten wachsenden Buchhandelsplattformen weltweit! Dank Print-On-Demand umwelt- und ressourcenschonend produziert.

Bücher schneller online kaufen
www.morebooks.shop